A Thousand Paths to Tranquillity

A Thousand Paths to
tranquillity

Sourcebooks, Inc.
Naperville, IL

David Baird

Contents

Introduction

In our hectic lives the pathway to the enchanted world of peace and tranquillity often eludes us. Perhaps we try too hard—we seek it here, we seek it there, and, hey presto! our lives become even less tranquil than before. It is often said that tranquillity lies in simple things—in reading a book, listening to a particular piece of music, walking through a gallery, or visiting a park. When life is stressful, just close your eyes and shut out the world for a few moments and allow yourself to recreate those tranquil moments. In the same way, the tranquil thoughts in this little book will create a kind of sanctuary when the pressures of life are unsurmountable and that secret garden of tranquillity seems so far away.

Tranquillity
Found

What is tranquillity and where can we find that low door in the garden wall that leads to it? We search for it frantically and never find it.

Tranquillity is not the same as laziness. Laziness is the habit of resting before you are tired.

Tranquillity is not with those who insist their lives have been destroyed by others. Those who know tranquillity take responsibility for their own lives.

Those who possess the capacity to not care about the praisers or fault finders will already have tranquillity in their heart.

Tranquillity is one of those things that is harder to find the more frantic your search for it. Relax and let it find you.

A tranquil mind
is paradise found.

The tranquil heart cares not what others think.

Fools complain, condemn, and criticize. Tranquillity belongs to those who can praise in others what they do right.

Speak of positive things.

Tranquillity does not lie in your worry about another's faults, it lies in your own self-improvement.

Stillness and tranquillity set things in order in the universe.

Tranquillity is beyond form,
it cannot be grasped and held.
It is beyond sound but perhaps
within sound, yet it cannot be
heard. It cannot be seen yet it
lies in everything we see.

Tranquillity often comes through trust.
He who does not trust enough will not
be trusted.

**Believe in yourself then you can
delight in tranquillity.**

The powers of wonder, curiosity, and delight are granted to the tranquil soul. Believe in yourself and all these will follow.

Tranquillity comes through listening. It is impossible to truly listen while doing something else at the same time.

There is tranquillity in freedom when the people are allowed to speak. There is tranquillity in democracy when the government listens.

There is tranquillity in wisdom. Wisdom comes through listening and the wise will, in turn, be listened to.

To pass on tranquillity to our children we must be careful of the things we say—for children *do* listen.

If you know how to listen tranquillity will speak to you.

If I could drop dead right now, I'd be the happiest man alive!

Samuel Goldwyn

Tranquillity comes when we can accept ourselves. For some it is reaching a point of accepting they are what they will always be and for others it is the point of deciding what it is they will become.

Tranquillity can be reached once you are able to accept that life is unlikely to go as you had planned.

Tranquillity is not the friend of those whose lives are spent yearning for the impossible.

Life is a series of concepts and ascribed significances. Tranquillity lies in recognizing and accepting that we made it that way.

While words are capable of twisting and turning our understanding of most philosophies and sciences, tranquillity is a touchstone of truth that governs words and reason.

Tranquillity comes as one masters understanding of the forces of nature and the world. The four seasons, the seas and their tides, the winds, and the transience of nature, growth, decay. Life in turmoil fights against these but once understood they are forces to be used.

Tranquillity is the meaning of meaning.

Tranquillity is often disrupted by becoming judgmental and attempting to improve upon nature using force.

Tranquillity can be reached by simply allowing the mind to become quiet.

You will only find tranquillity once you accept the need for a little self-examination in your life.

Tranquillity is reached by overcoming fear.

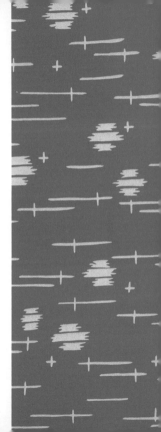

Face life with your natural mind—not your conditioned mind.

There are many paths to tranquillity, you don't have to adopt Zen or become Japanese to find it.

**Tranquillity is not created.
It is there in all of us already.
We simply lose touch with it.**

Tranquillity
is about being natural,
it's about being yourself
in all that you do.

Find tranquillity and you will find that you are special.

Tranquillity is the garden in which your soul can grow.

Tranquillity might at times leave you, but once found, you will always know the path by which to return.

A moment of tranquillity can relieve a lifetime of turmoil.

Tranquillity is not selfish, and neither is the friend who understands your need to go there.

Your route to tranquillity will be unlike the route taken by others.

Tranquillity is yours by right, like the air that you breathe.

There is enough tranquillity for everyone to enjoy but each must make their own journey.

Often, it is possible to find tranquillity by doing and saying nothing at all.

Finding tranquillity
gives you strength.

**Much turmoil is
created by those
who insist on taking
you "out of yourself"
while often the
tranquillity we seek
is only found by
getting inside
our self.**

More time is lost in trying to be punctual than is spent in tranquillity.

Ambition and tranquillity are not good bedfellows, but success and tranquillity are often discovered together.

We all seem so different and yet
only he who does not live in search
of happiness and tranquillity can
truly claim to be different.

**Imagine joy and you will discover
tranquillity. Discover living and you
will find joy.**

There is more life
to be discovered in
tranquillity than on
any busy street.

**Our tranquillity and
our happiness depend
upon ourselves.**

No matter who you are and how confused you are about life, there is one prayer that will provide the key to your tranquillity and it is simply to say "thank you."

You can find tranquillity with something to love, something to do, and something to hope for.

Tranquillity has many by-products, including happiness.

Sometimes, when we are too focused on ourselves and the turmoil we are in, tranquillity eludes us and we have to turn our attention away from ourselves momentarily.

A tranquil inner-spring runs through solitude, unpolluted and refreshing to the spirit.

It is important to realize that tranquillity is less of a destination than a manner of traveling.

Tranquillity is the place where you can let go of trying to become something and where you can concentrate upon being someone.

Tranquillity is often sought far off in the distance when it is right where you are and only you can grow it.

Nothing brings people together more quickly than laughter. Nothing guarantees tranquillity better than moments such as these.

Tranquillity serves to double our joy and in doing so divides our grief.

Tranquillity demands very little.

Tranquillity is a feeling and not a thought. One must try to feel and not think about feeling.

It is hard to find tranquillity where you are not understood, accepting this will bring some calm.

You have to make your mind up to seek tranquillity.

A tranquil mind gives you space to think.

There is a kind of tranquillity in the gratitude with which we greet life and all that's in it.

There are those who, when they are by themselves feel very alone. Those who know tranquillity feel less alone when they are by themselves.

There are those who know tranquillity and those who seem to others to know tranquillity.

By all means demand of life everything that it has to offer, but you will never discover tranquillity by demanding more than it has to give.

Tranquillity is a place for imaginative reflection, not a place of judgment.

Tranquillity is often lost in the search for it—we feel we cannot find it in ourselves and it seems impossible to locate it elsewhere.

There is tranquillity to be found in knowing that you are doing your best to make the most of yourself.

Tranquillity is beyond circumstances.

There is more tranquillity in being than in having.

Tranquillity is usually not to be found in any belief that focuses on the interest of one person, one group, or one race.

Tranquillity is a knowable natural flow. We will find it when we rediscover our spiritual nature.

Tranquillity is expressed in mellowness through all our actions and through our words.

Those who have found tranquillity are calm and pleasant to be with.

Tranquil people are willing people. They do not interfere in the lives of others.

Those who discover tranquillity can often help to guide others to their true nature and their own tranquillity.

Tranquillity comes by many names and forms. At root it is about a freely available, universal source of energy.

Many do not find tranquillity because of the terms used by those attempting to share it.

To seek tranquillity in an organized group can be helpful, but to many this method can put up even more barriers between the searcher and tranquillity.

No one holds a monopoly
on tranquillity.

Tranquillity does not
come as a reward
for sacrifice.

Often the most opening
advice is to be found from
those closest to us.

**Some find tranquillity by
contemplating the infinite,
while others seek and find
it by focusing upon the
small and intricate.**

Tranquillity is known by many
to be a great antidote to pain.

Tranquillity does
not discriminate—
no one is chosen,
no one is rejected.

**It is difficult,
if not impossible,
for the selfish
and the suspicious
to discover
tranquillity.**

No barrier can prevent those whose life-wish is to find tranquillity from reaching their goal.

The quest for tranquillity is not a religious belief. It is for anybody and everybody and that includes you.

To reach tranquillity it is vital to have an unclouded perception.

Tranquillity is not seen, it just IS.

Without desire the heart becomes quiet, the whole world is made tranquil.

To begin our journey on the path to tranquillity we must first arrive at a level where everything is in harmony.

To arrive at harmony we must travel toward our natural spiritual energy and allow it to meet us, our mind, our body our surroundings, our lives.

Tranquillity helps us to know when to follow the heart and when to follow the mind.

Once tranquillity has been reached there will no longer be a divorce from your inner energy and your daily life.

Those who find tranquillity are gentle, non-violent, and respectful of the gift they possess.

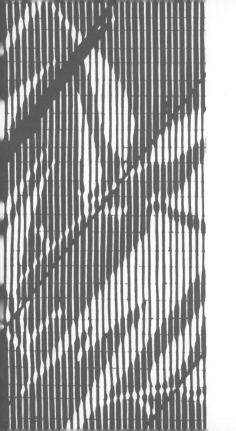

**Tranquillity
can only be
found when
you begin
to manage
yourself well.**

Tranquillity
is to be
reached
by working
toward
a spiritual
evolution.

Everyone makes mistakes but tranquillity comes to those who consistently educate themselves to come closer into harmony with spiritual nature.

To find tranquillity is to come home.

Find tranquillity in the morning just after rising, in the evening just before sleep.

Tranquillity, faith, and personal behavior are one—they cannot be divorced from each other.

We fluctuate long between love and hatred before we arrive at tranquillity.

Tranquillity is already there in your loveliest and purest thoughts.

Tranquillity lies in the beauty that forms in your mind.

Tranquillity sustains you from the inside.

Life cannot be interpreted perfectly without discovering tranquillity.

The kingdom of tranquillity already lies within you.

Tranquillity is what no eye has seen
and what no ear has heard. What no
hand has touched and what has
never occurred to the human mind.

From tranquillity emerges
a person brimming over with
self-reliance and contentment.

**Tranquillity comes to those
who know themselves.**

Tranquillity breeds the ability to disagree with what others say. The calm listener understands exactly what it is he is disagreeing with.

Tranquillity can be reached by taking no action.

There is more tranquillity to be found by creating opportunities than by going off in search of them.

We all live in the same hectic world—some of us deal with it better than others.

Some of us have tranquillity in our lives—some of us will never allow it into our lives.

We all need to be able to understand and be understood. Without this there can be no tranquillity.

We are the ones
who block our own
paths to tranquillity
and we are the ones
who must clear
them again.

Voices of Calm

What is the product
of virtue? Tranquillity.
Epictetus

**Humor is emotional chaos
remembered in tranquillity.**
James Thurber

When one has the feeling of dislike for evil, when one feels tranquil, one finds pleasure in listening to good teachings; when one has these feelings and appreciates them, one is free of fear.

Buddha

They who live have all things; they who withhold have nothing.

Hindu proverb

Those who are
free of resentful
thoughts surely
find peace.

Buddha

**There is no joy
but calm.**

Tennyson

No man is more cheated than a selfish man.

Henry Ward Beecher

A happy life consists in tranquillity of mind.

Cicero

The ideal of beauty is
simplicity and tranquillity.

Goethe

**I love tranquil solitude
And such society
As is quiet, wise, and good.**

Shelley

If the thoughts are absolutely tranquil the heavenly heart can be seen. The heavenly heart lies between sun and moon (i.e. between the two eyes). It is the home of the inner light.

Lu Yen

The heavy is the root of the light.
The tranquil is the ruler of the hasty.

Lao Tzu

The reasonable man adapts
himself to the world; the
unreasonable one persists
in trying to adapt the world
to himself. Therefore all
progress depends on the
unreasonable man.

George Bernard Shaw

In pursuit, even of the best things, we ought to be calm and tranquil.

Cicero

Tranquil pleasures last the longest; we are not fitted to bear the long burden of great joy.

Henry Ward Beecher

How calm, how beautiful comes on
The still hour, when storms have gone,
When warring winds have died away
And clouds, beneath the dancing ray
Melt off and leave the land and sea,
Sleeping in bright tranquillity.

Thomas Moore

Mistake not. Those pleasures are not pleasures that trouble the quiet and tranquillity of thy life.

Jeremy Taylor

The only path to a tranquil life
is through virtue.

Juvenal

**Power is so characteristically calm,
that calmness in itself has the
aspect of power.**

Bulwer-Lytton

When young, rejoice in the tranquillity
of the old. However great your glory,
be forbearing in your manner. Boast not
of what you know, even when learned.
However high may you rise, be not proud.

Nagarjuna

**Calmness and irony are the only
weapons worthy of the strong.**

I Ching

Remember to preserve a calm soul amid difficulties.

Horace

An eager pursuit of fortune is inconsistent with a severe devotion to truth.
The heart must grow tranquil before the thought can become searching.

Bovee

Those who seek the true path to enlightenment must not expect an easy task or one made pleasant by offers of respect and honor and devotion. And further, they must not aim with a slight effort, at a trifling advance in calmness or knowledge or insight.

Buddha

If speaking is silver, then listening is gold.

Turkish proverb

It is the disease of not listening,
the malady of not marking,
that I am troubled withal.

William Shakespeare

**Only the wisest and stupidest of
men never change.**

Confucius

Once the self does not exist,
How could the *mine* exist?

Nagarjuna

Ne'er saw I, never felt, a calm so deep!
The river glideth at his own sweet will:
Dear God! the very houses seem asleep:
And all that mighty heart is lying still!

William Wordsworth

**It is the province of knowledge to
speak and it is the privilege of
wisdom to listen.**

Oliver Wendell Holmes

You must be the change
you wish to see in the world.

Mahatma Ghandi

Listening is a magnetic and strange thing, a creative force. The friends who listen to us are the ones we move toward. When we are listened to, it creates us, makes us unfold and expand.

Karl Menninger

In nature things move violently to their place, and calmly in their place.

Francis Bacon

Surely there is something in the unruffled calm of nature that overawes our little anxieties and doubts: the sight of the deep-blue sky, and the clustering stars above, seem to impart a quiet in the mind.

Jonathan Edwards

In the mountains the shortest way is from peak to peak: but for that one must have long legs.

Friedrich Nietzsche

All intelligent thoughts have already been thought; what is necessary is only to try to think them again.

Goethe

Nothing is more damaging to
a new truth than an old error.

Goethe

**The distinction between past,
present, and future is only a
stubbornly persistent illusion.**

Albert Einstein

I have had a dream, past the wit of man
to say what dream it was.

William Shakespeare

If the doors of perception were cleansed everything would appear to man as it is, infinite.

William Blake

We dance round in a ring and suppose. But the Secret sits in the middle and knows.

Robert Frost

**Patience is so like Fortitude,
that she seems either her sister
or her daughter.**

Aristotle

From out of all the many
particulars comes oneness,
and out of oneness come
all the many particulars.

Heraclitus

Time does not relinquish its rights,
either over human beings or over
mountains.

Goethe

We shall not cease from exploration
And the end of all our exploring
Will be to arrive where we started
And know the place for the first time.

T. S. Eliot

Whereof one cannot speak, thereof one must be silent.

Wittgenstein

Words plainly force and
overrule the understanding,
and throw all into confusion,
and lead men away into
innumerable and inane
controversies and fancies.

Francis Bacon

It is the theory that decides what can be observed.

Albert Einstein

The highest happiness of man … is to have probed what is knowable and quietly to revere what is unknowable.

Goethe

Everything should be made as simple as possible, but not simpler.
Albert Einstein

The good and the wise lead quiet lives.
Euripides

You can discover more about
a person in an hour of play
than in a year of conversation.

Plato

**Different men seek after happiness
in different ways and by different
means, and so make for themselves
different modes of life and forms
of government.**

Aristotle

And what if in your dream you went
to heaven and there you plucked
a strange and beautiful flower;
and what if when you awoke
you had the flower in your hand?
Oh, what then?

Samuel Taylor Coleridge

In order to draw a limit to
thinking, we should have to
think both sides of this limit.

Wittgenstein

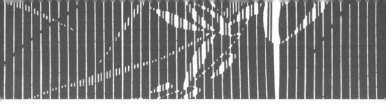

The reason angels can fly
is that they take themselves
so lightly.

G. K. Chesterton

**Put your heart, mind, intellect and
soul even to your smallest acts.
This is the secret of success.**

Swami Sivanda

When you are sorrowful look again in your heart, and you shall see that in truth you are weeping for that which has been your delight.

Kahlil Gibran

Patience is the support of weakness, impatience is the ruin of strength.

Colton

Patience and time
do more than
strength or passion.
La Fontaine

Your body is precious.
It is your vehicle for awakening.
Treat it with care.

Buddha

Cheerfulness keeps up a kind of daylight in the mind, and fills it with a steady and perpetual serenity.

Joseph Addison

The purpose of our lives is to be happy.

Dalai Lama

**Peace comes from within.
Do not seek it without.**

Buddha

Anger blows out
the lamp of the mind.

Robert Ingersoll

Flowers feed the soul.
Mohammed

Drag your thoughts away from your troubles ... by the ears, by the heels, or any other way you can manage it.
Mark Twain

Life is too important to take seriously.

Oscar Wilde

**Health is the greatest gift,
contentment the greatest wealth,
faithfulness the best relationship.**

Buddha

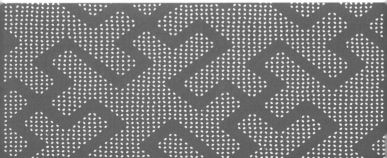

We are never so happy or unhappy as we think.

Rochefoucauld

In every man's heart there is a secret nerve that answers to the vibrations of beauty.

Christopher Morley

**Neither fire nor wind,
birth nor death can erase
our good deeds.**

Buddha

In the middle of difficulty lies
opportunity.

Albert Einstein

**Those in a hurry do
not arrive.**

Zen saying

We must believe in luck. For how else can we explain the success of those we don't like?

Jean Cocteau

Patience is the art of hoping.

Vauvenargues

If you pursue evil with pleasure, the pleasure passes away and the evil remains; If you pursue good with labor, the labor passes away but the good remains.

Cicero

A person in danger should not try to escape at one stroke. He should first calmly hold his own, then be satisfied with small gains, which will come by creative adaptations.

I Ching

Old age has a great sense of calm and freedom. When the passions have relaxed their hold and have escaped, not from one master, but from many.

Plato

Everything comes
if a man will only wait.

Tancred

A smooth and steadfast mind,
Gentle thoughts and calm desires,
Hearts with equal love combined,
Kindle never-dying fires.

Thomas Carew

What is deservedly suffered
must be borne with calmness,
but when the pain is unmerited
the grief is resistless.

Ovid

Richer is one hour of repentance and good works in this world than all of life of the world to come; and richer is one hour's calm of spirit in the world to come than all of life of this world.

The Talmud

Remember to preserve a calm soul amid difficulties.

Horace

Think with the whole body.

Taisen Deshimaru

Patience is the key to contentment.
Mohammed

True courage is cool and calm. The bravest of men have the least of a brutal, bullying insolence and in the very time of danger are found the most serene and free.

Shaftesbury III

Patience is bitter but its fruit is sweet.

Rousseau

We are such stuff
As dreams are made on,
And our little life
Is rounded with a sleep.

William Shakespeare

The patient in spirit is better than the proud in spirit.

Ecclesiastes

A man who as a physical being is always turned toward the outside, thinking that his happiness lies outside him, finally turns inward and discovers that the source is within him.

Kierkegaard

Love is eternal—the aspect may change, but not the essence … love makes one calmer about many things, and that way, one is more fit for one's work.

Vincent Van Gogh

How poor are they that have not patience!
What wound did ever heal but by degrees?

William Shakespeare

To see a world in a grain of sand,
And Heaven in a wild flower,
Hold Infinity in the palm of your hand,
And Eternity in an hour.

William Blake

A dry soul is wisest and best.

Heraclitus

Have much and be confused.

Tao te Ching

There is one form of hope which is never unwise, and which certainly does not diminish with the increase of knowledge. In that form it changes its name, and we call it patience.

Bulwer-Lytton

People only see what they are prepared to see.

Ralph Waldo Emerson

One never goes so far as when one doesn't know where one is going.

Goethe

The way up and the way down are one and the same.

Heraclitus

Those who cannot remember the past are condemned to repeat it.

George Santayana

With time and patience the mulberry leaf becomes silk.

Chinese proverb

Blessed is he who carries within himself a god, an ideal, and obeys it.

Louis Pasteur

Patience is the best remedy for every trouble.

Plautus

Politeness is to human nature
what warmth is to wax.

Arthur Schopenhauer

**Self-confidence is the first requisite
to great undertakings.**

Samuel Johnson

We are what we
repeatedly do.
Aristotle

The wisest of the wise may err.
Aeschylus

The good people sleep much better at night than the bad people. Of course, the bad people enjoy the waking hours much more.

Woody Allen

Seek not the things that are too hard for thee, neither search the things that are beyond thy strength.

Apocrypha

Dignity does not consist in possessing honors, but in deserving them.

Aristotle

In those whom I like, I can find no common denominator; in those whom I love I can: they all make me laugh.

W. H. Auden

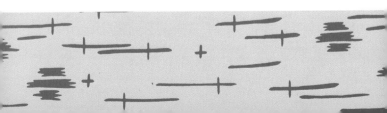

Do not correct a scoffer, lest he hate you; rebuke a wise man and he will love you. Give instruction to a wise man and he will be wiser still; teach a just man and he will increase in learning.

Proverb

I think; therefore I am.

Descartes

Slight not what's near, when aiming at what's far.

Euripides

Life is what happens to you while you're busy making other plans.

John Lennon

Do not fear to be eccentric in opinion, for every opinion now accepted was once eccentric.

Bertrand Russell

Let him that would move the world first move himself.

Socrates

There is
nothing
permanent
except
change.

Heraclitus

Think for
yourselves and
let others enjoy
the privilege to
do so, too.

Voltaire

If you want 1 year of prosperity, grow grain.
If you want 10 years of prosperity, grow trees.
If you want 100 years of prosperity, grow people.

Chinese proverb

We are not separate from spirit. We are in it

Plotinus

Act without doing; work without effort.

Tao te Ching

Those things that hurt, instruct.

Benjamin Franklin

Mind is locked in matter like the spirit Ariel in a cloven pine. Like Ariel, men struggle to escape the drag of the matter they inhabit.

Loren Eiseley

When the mind is
possessed of reality,
it feels tranquil and joyous
even without music
or song, and it produces
a pure fragrance even
without incense or tea.

Hung Tzu-ch'eng

Calm

The calm person is far more sociable and civilized than those who try to live rigorously by laws and watchwords.

Tension is destructive— calm aids healing.

Fear breeds tension.

Although honest people are cheated daily, calm people are honest regardless.

Calm is the master of haste.

**Acting in haste
can lead us to
lose control.**

Calm and quiet have
the power to
overcome the world.

**Sit and be calm,
if you want to, cry.**

Go to the sea—its ebb and flow are like our own unrest.

Go to the pond—its stillness lies within each of us.

Tranquillity begins at the water's edge.

The
stillness
that
follows
laughter is
like having
a great
weight
removed
from your
shoulders.

Many in this world are known more by what they despise than who they think they are.

Facts do not cease to exist just because we choose to ignore them.

Security does not exist in nature— accept this and return to calm.

Before taking action, we must ask ourselves: "Is there more danger to come from avoiding danger than from exposing ourselves to danger?"

There is no wrong time
to do the right thing.

**The future, no matter
how threatening it may
appear, can only come
one day at a time.**

The tranquillity of others can
help us to become calm.

We are only so unhappy because
we insist on believing that the whole
reason of life is happiness.

Learn to accept
those things you
cannot alter, not
blindly, but with full
understanding.

Learn to manage
your stress.

Keep tropical fish.

Stop dancing on the edge
of the volcano.

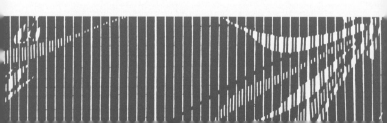

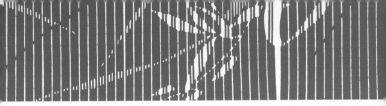

Avoid the path that leads to the triple heart bypass.

When you see a bird in flight allow your eyes to fly with it—admire it.

Taste the day.

**Learn to really
listen with
your ears—and
your eyes.**

When you breathe,
fill your body with air.
When you exhale,
empty yourself of air.

**Try to conceptualize;
a chair can be a boat,
a bed can be a glider.
Play, relax, and enjoy.**

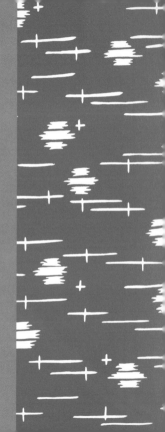

Sing the song of being alive.

Write anything—
a few words,
a thought, a poem,
a letter.

Do nothing and be brave
about it.

Take pleasure in the art of living—dine, really dine; prepare, cook, and eat.

Pray—even to nature—openly, be yourself.

**Learn to love another
unconditionally.**

Wonder at the
wonder of it all.

**Allow yourself to
get lost in the forest
of your imagination.**

Celebrate life quietly.

There is more punishment to be had "by" our sins than we are likely to receive "for" our sins.

Dig yourself a pit and you're likely to fall into it.

The main problem with lying is that liars rarely find themselves able to believe anyone else.

Walk the internal path that leads to peace.

Jealousy is one of the biggest forms of self-torment that exists.

If we set out to elicit the very best
in others we will bring out the best
in ourselves.

**Depression has a knack of
feeding on itself, but cannot live
in a calm heart.**

Doubt breeds doubt,
calm breeds calm.

**At the root of man's inhumanity
to fellow man lies indifference.**

We who are not blind,
why do we refuse to see?
We who are not ignorant,
why do we refuse to know?

**The majority of living, breathing
human beings, spend the majority
of their lives trying not to think.**

Nothing endures like truth,
even if lies are quicker initially.

**It is not worth the stress of getting
angry unless you can be absolutely
certain that you are angry at the
right person, at the right time, to
the right level, and for absolutely
the right reason.**

Turn your envy into admiration.

The truly great will go out of their way to help others to become so. Those who have failed themselves will do everything in their power to suffocate ambition.

Allow someone to make you hate them and they have won, and it is you that will suffer.

Learn to find joy in the simple things, the quiet things, and the things which come free.

A calm mind is a healthy mind.

Choose to be calm. It *is* an option.

It is not quick or easy to achieve calm. It is an ongoing lesson.

Relax your mind and let your senses come alive.

Remember to breathe not weak, snatched gasps, but deep reviving drafts.

Calm doesn't mean shutting yourself away from life, it means finding a truer, deeper understanding of life's problems.

No matter how rough the waves on the ocean surface, the waters beneath are always calm.

Let tension go, feel your brow relax and the worries flow away.

Try to see again—really see—like a child.

Having a calm mind is being able to choose how to react.

Don't feel guilty about making things easy for yourself.

When you can, allow yourself to turn away from stressful situations.

He that is angry is seldom at ease.

Calm is ruined by impatience.

Calm is the sister of patience and patience is the parent of hope.

The proud live large,
the calm live long.

**Be calm and everything
will come.**

Calmness
heals much.

The calm can always conquer
the impatient.

**Calm is the strongest weapon
against misfortune.**

Without calm all roads
look too long.

**Without calm all honors seem
beyond our grasp.**

Unless there is calm there can be no success.

Compassion fills the heart.

In nature there is no storm that is not followed by calm.

Calmness gives us the patience to do small things to perfection and the skill to tackle the difficult with ease.

In moments of extreme panic, turn to those who can remain calm, for their thinking remains uncluttered and objective.

Show me a genius and therein you will find calm.

Calm is the gateway to paradise that the impatient can never pass through.

To achieve calm,
we require patience.

We can find calm when we agree within ourselves to bear what cannot be altered.

Courage opens the heart.

Learn to accept that what cannot be cured must be endured.

Calmness itself is a great healer.

Calmness is ours if we choose to adopt the pace of nature, for nature's secret is her patience.

Calm must first be initiated from within us, to seek it without is nearly impossible.

When we can face reality in a calm way, then the mind can feel tranquil.

To be calm is to have self-control.

Those who can remain calm have their own private pace with which to meet misfortune and fortune unperplexed.

You will not be able to take control of your life until you can take control of yourself.

Calm is the clock
during the
thunderstorm.

**Contemplate that
which is dearest to
your heart for that
is the seed of calm.**

Those who can travel
this life calmly,
unattached, and
unrepulsed by objects
and events, will win
eternal peace.

Dualism destroys calmness, but we can be serene in the oneness of things if we are patient and concentrate.

**Cultivate calm
in the garden of
your heart.**

The weeds that choke
the garden of calm are
jealousy, selfishness,
greed, hatred, and
impatience.

**Enjoy the calm
that comes in
the still moments
after the storms
have subsided.**

Arise calmly and live the day in tranquillity.

To remain calm we must not fight against enforced entanglements. Our entanglements must be calmly borne.

Enter into calm contemplation. Quiet meditation distinguishes the seeker of enlightenment.

Only by getting to know our self through reflection and meditation can we reach our spirit and achieve calm.

There is more calm to be had from contemplating a day simply spent than from reliving battles and victories, successes and triumphs.

**Truth is always the companion
of calm.**

So calm is quiet contemplation
that it is hard to be drawn out
from it.

**Solitude is the best vehicle
for calm.**

There is great calm in genius
and solitude.

When our inner sound can kill the outer sound we will have reached the calmness wherein tranquillity may be found.

Cope.
Avoid stress.
Live for stability.
Embrace change.
Be calm in the face of fortune and adversity.

Our difficulty in remaining calm seems to stem from the fact that few of us actually like and trust ourselves.

A life where there is no time to be calm and reflect is not really a life.

The point of it all is to be able to control your own mind to focus on what is most important to you.

Remember, all life is transient, grasp this and greed and anger will be replaced with calm and tranquillity.

Any dissatisfaction we may have with ourselves will upset calm. Do not allow yourself to fall under the power of confused emotions.

Calmly consider the rationality of your actions. Just because you have been scalded once does not mean that all water is to be feared.

A life without calm is a life without soul.
A life without soul is like an empty sack.
An empty sack cannot stand upright.

It is the nature of a great mind to be calm and undisturbed.

There is no tranquillity to be had where there is no desire to calmly examine one's life.

Mankind chooses, it seems, to be in turmoil, and periods of tranquillity are few and far between, even avoided by many as unfashionable.

The most vital time to relax is when you don't have time for it.

A calm heart is
a free heart.

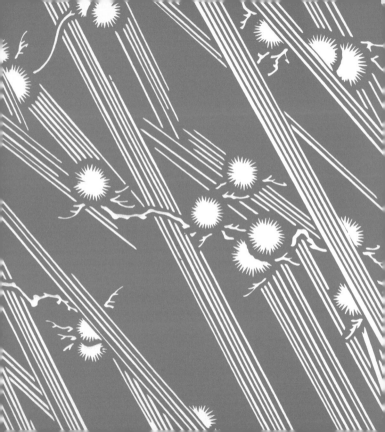

Patience

Be competent in your daily life, and in all your actions. Allow yourself to be aware of the time and the season.

Listening is not always easy.

No two people will see life in exactly the same way.

It is wise to speak your truth quietly and clearly.

Many big plans have been ruined by a little impatience.

Listen to others, no matter how dull or ignorant they seem, for everyone has their story.

It is as important to be patient with yourself as it is to have self-discipline.

You don't have to be the winner to take part.

Success begins with will.

Intelligent people have the ability to control their emotions using little more than reason.

Work is the price of success.

In the space of one lifetime you may not know all that the world has to offer.

Endurance is a form of concentrated patience.

It is impossible to expect the world to stand still and share your grief.

Take time to discover the best in others.

It is as important to enjoy your planning as it is to celebrate your achievements.

It takes a lifetime to become the person we want to be.

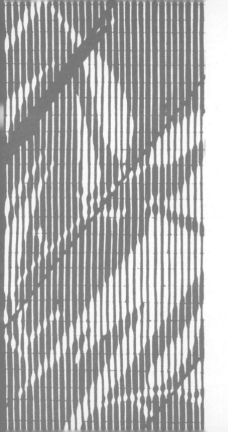

Patience
overcomes
all things.

**We will
recognize
patience
when we
do not
attempt to
interfere
with the
future.**

Rain will fall—we cannot make it so.

Listening is often the best means of persuasion.

Ask and listen and you will learn.

When you listen to somebody attentively, you listen not only to the words, but also to the feeling of what is being conveyed, to the whole of it, not part of it.

A quiet mind is the best cure for a low mood.

Quiet is listening without judgment.

Compatibility comes about not through sameness but through respect for our differences.

Focus yourself upon what is and not the shoulds and should nots of life.

Patience is a gift, but it is possible to learn it.

So much of the turmoil in our lives is the product of imagined ideas about how some other person thinks or feels.

If you set about doing something, put your heart into it and enjoy it, that way, regardless of the outcome, it will be a positive experience.

To feel loved, give love.

To be patient with another is to show simple human courtesy.

We are rarely free in this life. We allow ourselves to become slaves to fashion, slaves to the image, slaves to thoughts and sensations. All these are dams to the flow of our natural thought processes.

Are we ourselves or some shallow imitation of others who we would like to be?

Do not try to be all things to everyone. Be content to be yourself to yourself.

Allow yourself time to return to the unconditioned, the uncreated state of mind and being.

Whatever people try to tell you, don't be fooled by them. Don't accept other people's delusions.

We can lift ourselves out of ignorance, all it takes is perseverance.

Life consists of
the unknown and
the unknowable.

**Begin by knowing that you
have already arrived.**

True law leads to freedom.

Learn not to rely completely on any other human beings—we meet all life's greatest tests alone.

Cherish your dreams, for if your dreams die life becomes a wingless bird.

There are two kinds of dreams: those we dream by night (from which we wake to find they were not real); and those we dream by day (which we can act upon to make possible).

**Hold on to your dreams, allow
yourself the luxury of time to make
them come true.**

It is better to try to be something
to someone than to try and be
everything to everybody and fail.

**Enjoy the smile that the flower
gives now, for with time it will
surely die.**

There is only hesitancy until one commits. Providence can only be freed by committing.

Do not fear to open the doors that lie between what is known and what is unknown.

To go through life filled with self-pity is rather like carrying your canoe across the river.

Chase butterflies and they will never be caught, watch butterflies and they will come to you.

Between the question and the answer lies free choice.

The most important habit to acquire in this life is happiness.

Let your heart light your way.

The search for tranquillity is a lifetime's quest. It cannot be hurried.

Patience facilitates calm.

**Tackle a job with impatience
and it will take twice as long.**

The day is
brightened
with a smile.

Success and happiness taste better when shared.

Nothing will exist to one who insists on keeping their eyes closed tight.

Patience is the key to paradise.

Sit quietly,
doing nothing,
spring comes,
and the grass
grows by
itself.

Zen saying

There is nothing finer than resting after doing nothing — laziness is resting before doing nothing.

If you can spend a perfectly useless afternoon in a perfectly useless manner, you have learned how to live.

Lin Yutang

While man complicates his life, every other creature is busy enjoying it.

We can hope for little more in life than to learn how to live.

It is unlikely any of us will avoid pain—but whether we suffer or not seems to be more a matter of individual choice.

We all stand in the midst of eternity. Now.

Time will not
be hurried.

**Let the flower you hold
in your hand be your
world for that moment.**

Slow down and enjoy life.

While fashion strives to make us all the same, life succeeds in making sure we're all different.

Fun is the sacred right of everyone.

Even the most ordinary among us are quite extraordinary.

The aim of life is to live, take a deep breath, and begin.

Wonder is the beginning of understanding.

Where there is delight there is little concern for effort.

There can be no rainbows without rain.

Next time you are greeted with "How do you do?" consider your response; the rest of your life hinges on it.

There are those who go through life impatiently waiting for something to happen so that they can start living. And there are those that accept each day as a precious and original gift to be enjoyed.

Don't wish your life away. Impatience is the enemy of tranquillity.

Pleasure denied remains pleasure sought.

Impatience drives us on, and is apt to drive us over our goal without us noticing.

Put off your anger until you can't find a reason to be angry.

All things come to he who has patience.

Never underestimate yourself, for the world will insist on taking you at face value.

Take time to laugh,
it is the most
powerful medicine
on earth.

**Life is filled with detours,
the secret is to enjoy the
scenery.**

True compassion is the swiftest path to tranquillity.

Don't be too busy to experience joy.

One generation's tragedy often becomes the next generation's comedy, so you might as well start laughing about it now.

Don't ask others what they think unless you are prepared to listen.

What will you do with your moment of good fortune?

An ounce of patience is worth more than a pound of ambition.

Who is the richer, he who has much and wants more or he who has little and wants less?

Collect all the pretty shells from the beach and you will destroy the beauty that was that beach.

Consider your feelings and temperament as your seasons and weather. Fair will follow foul and the sun will come out eventually.

You might feel you know your mind but do you know your heart as well?

Look up and be one with the sky, but don't tread in anything nasty while your mind is elsewhere.

The little things in life are generally the most important.

When considering how to spend your day, think about being asked in years to come how you spent your life.

Life is a
matter of
moments,
don't be
in a hurry
for it to
be over.

Adopt the pace of nature.

Consider a curve that can set everything else straight and smile.

The past cannot be changed by you and worrying about the future will only serve to ruin your present.

Why spend your life
worrying about the future—
you will know it when
it comes.

**It is far better to understand a little
than to misunderstand a lot.**

Man's honesty does not increase with wealth, rather the contrary is true.

Honesty is
a state of mind.

Take the time to get to know others before you complain that no one understands you.

Remember, we all carry with us the spiritual energy which we were born with. Be careful not to crush yours under the weight of expectation.

Through conditioning,
both physical and mental,
we become separated
from our natural energy.

**Nature is infinitely patient,
infinitely calm. Everything comes,
everything passes.**

When we are able to know that there is no longer any separation between the spirit, the body, and the mind, we will have reached our destination.

Enjoy the richness of the world.

None of us are doomed.

Each and every one of us has the opportunity to accept the responsibility for our own development.

The world is filled with people waiting for some miracle to improve the state of things and while they wait their own responsibilities are neglected.

A patient heart
will not be
disappointed.

How do we protect the truth of ourselves in a world that seems to require us to never be who and what we are?

It is fine to gaze up at the stars, but don't trample all the daisies underfoot.

We each attract certain energies—some positive, some negative—to us without being aware of it. From time to time we must focus on the kind of energy we want to attract.

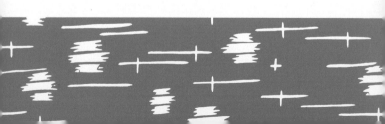

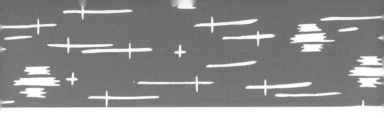

Salvation does not come ready packaged.

Those who will discourage us from seeking tranquillity are those who will never attempt such a journey in their own lives.

What is the mind if the heart is blind?

Be still,
be patient—
that is the
greatest
strength
we know.

Contentment

Those
who
know
do not
talk.

A tranquil heart is a happy heart.

When you come to know you have enough then you will be rich.

Tranquillity is an attitude of mind.

Take time to care for those around you.

It is foolish to constantly compare your own happiness with that of others, contentment denies comparison.

Realize now that money is not the reason for living.

You will discover that sometimes when you fall those that you would least expect help you up again.

True friendship continues to grow regardless of distance or obstacles.

When you begin to trust, others will begin to care.

The most important moment to be cherished is always now.

Your dreams and visions are to be cherished. They are messengers from your soul.

Discover peace in silence. You will learn that it is possible to journey through the haste and noise of life to placidity.

It is far more fulfiling just to be yourself than to waste your life trying to be something you are not.

Take time to see the humor in life.

Sudden misfortune hits us all from time to time. Nurture strength of spirit now, this will help to shield you.

Loneliness and fatigue breed fear—it is better not to trouble yourself with your own imaginings.

It is important to win the affection and respect of children as much as that of grown-ups.

Play is the secret of perpetual youth.

It is far more satisfying to live for progress than for perfection.

Reading is the foundation of wisdom, always make time for a book.

Learn to value your time alone—when you value something you are keener to protect it.

A goal is only as worthy as the effort that's required to achieve it.

Winners are people just like you.

The great essentials of happiness are something to do, something to care for, and something to hope for.

Why should your dreams not be beautiful? Why should you not believe in your dreams?

It is better to give up trying to get people to love you and to concentrate on becoming somebody who others can love.

You will discover that no matter how much you care, you will never receive the same amount of care in return—do not expect it.

Trust is something that takes years to build and seconds to destroy.

Remember to be gentle with yourself and others.

A lifetime of heartache can be created in an instant.

We are responsible for how we feel.

Every time you feel discouraged with life remember that nobody got to where they are today without beginning where they were yesterday.

Every heart has its own ache.

Restless thoughts are as dangerous to a tranquil mind as a swarm of hornets.

There are many paths to tranquillity, travel that which suits you.

To appreciate the beauty of the flower you must not pick it petal by petal.

It is the same moon that is reflected in the puddles as in the fountains.

Remove anxiety, remove boredom, remove angst.

Consider
the candle—
the brighter
it lights others
the faster it
consumes
itself.

A good conscience
is a soft pillow.

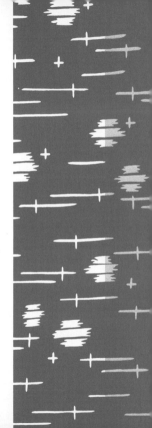

Time is important. It is vital to use some of it to be alone.

Peace and enlightenment are your right.

DREAM BIG.

Things worth doing seldom come easy.

You will discover that there will be good days, and there will be bad days. For you, for me, and for everyone else. You are never alone.

When you can recognize what you can see, and that which is hidden from you, then things will become plain to you.

**When we are not content
we are lost.**

Whoever has ears to hear,
let him hear.

You are your own master.

We are not defiled by what goes into our mouth so much as that which issues from our mouth.

Why do we seek the answer to the end when we haven't yet found the answer to the beginning?

We are all of us merely passers-by.

Is it possible to love the tree and hate the fruit?

Grapes are not harvested from thorns, figs gathered from thistles, and contentment will not be found in an angry heart.

None was born to lower their eyes in the presence of others.

**A good man brings forth good,
an evil man brings forth evil.
We each have the capacity for
both within us.**

It is impossible for a man to stretch two
bows. And it is impossible for a servant
to serve two masters. Decide what it is
that you want and do not be distracted.

**If mankind can move mountains
it should not be so difficult to
make peace.**

To experience
without abstraction
is to sense the world.
To experience with
abstraction is to know
the world.

**When you realize
the tranquillity
within, you and
your relationship
with the world
will flourish.**

Be in harmony with nature,
do not always swim against
the tide.

**Be in harmony with nature,
nature does not possess
fear and without fear,
the heart may be quiet.**

**Be in harmony with nature,
nature does not possess
hate and without hate,
the heart may be quiet.**

Be in harmony with nature,
nature does not possess
envy and without envy,
the heart may be quiet.

Work at being happy, it is the most worthwhile exercise.

We must never hope to perceive anything fully or comprehend anything completely.

Friendliness is the road to happiness.

With a tranquil heart you can see beauty on bleak days.

You can't think your way into a new way of living—you have to live your way into a new way of thinking.

Don't let the memory of past failures deter you from future success.

It is not important just that we can see, it is how far we can see and what we see that matters.

It is not important just that we can hear, it is how much we can hear and what we hear that matters.

It is not important just that we can feel, it is how we feel and how we interpret our feelings that matters.

To deny the existence of the unconscious suggests that we know completely everything there is to be known about the psyche.

We can never hope to know all there is to know about any individual, least of all ourselves.

It is possible to isolate part of the mind to keep it calm in a sea of worries, and to return to this safe harbor at will.

We all have the tendency to erect psychological barriers to protect us against anything new or unknown.

Once discovered, tranquillity will continue to influence our conscious minds.

Forgetting is a normal process of self-protection.

Learn to be content with what you have, peace comes from not wanting.

The mind can only keep a few images in full focus at one time, and even these tend to grow foggy with time.

Many people mistakenly overestimate the role of will power and think that nothing can influence their minds that they do not intend to.

Learn to differentiate between the intentional and unintentional contents of the mind.

Some of the world's best ideas owe their existence to inspirations from the unconscious.

True contentment is quiet.

The harder you search for contentment,
the less likely you are to find it.

Life consists of a complex
of opposites: birth and death;
happiness and misery;
day and night; good and evil.

We need meaning in our life, we need
to find a meaningful place for ourselves
in the vast complexity of the universe.

**Until we allow ourselves to find
some kind of meaning to our lives
we will feel lost and miserable.**

When people lose the meaning of their
lives they effectively stop living.

If we cannot live in harmony with external nature, then we will find it difficult to understand our own natures.

Nobody can afford to wait for somebody else to do what he is loath to do himself.

Don't be afraid to dream.

Do not allow your quest for tranquillity to become so enormous that you become overwhelmed at the mere thought of it.

Modern man gives way to impulses that do not belong to him at all.

Tranquillity is not a retreat from reality.

When you point at the sky, don't mistake your fingernail for the moon.

To see clearly, your mind must be free from wandering words and from the floating fantasies of memory.

When you feel yourself becoming too wrapped up in yourself, go outside and gaze up at a starry sky.

The personal ego, interests, and preferences are nothing more than traps which will alienate man from the natural entirety of universal life.

Help another and you help yourself.

Understanding is the root of harmony and tranquillity.

Always endeavor to
develop harmonious
relationships with
all people.

**The teacher is there
to help the student's
growth, the student
has a duty to accept
the teacher's help.**

One cannot gain
complete knowledge
with only a partial
view of life.

Tranquillity is hard to find for those who rush too quickly into accepting and believing whatever others tell them.

To enjoy the highs of life one must also have tasted the lows.

Don't ever give up. Have the courage of your convictions.

Do not set your goals too high, or you will fail before you have begun.

Why is the present called the present? Because it is a gift.

We all have problems we have to deal with, no one leads a trouble-free life, but it is how we deal with these problems that makes the difference.

To the outside view, a contented person may look very much like a discontented person.

You are the sum total of the choices you make.

Anything inside you that immobilizes you, gets in your way, and keeps you from your goals is part of you and is yours to dispose of as you wish.

**Take some risks
and stop worrying.**

Expect
to stay
healthy.

**Take charge of your
feelings and regain
control of your life.**

People who panic or get depressed usually do so because they have lost control.

A diamond is
a chunk of coal
that made good
under pressure.

He who laughs, lasts.

Invest a little of your time in looking after your body as well as your mind.

Consciousness naturally resists anything unconscious and unknown.

Every day, reserve a little time, just for yourself, and relax.

Contentment is within everyone's grasp, it is simply being satisfied with what you have made of your life, and feeling in control of how you feel.

Perception

When somebody actually listens to us, it creates us, it makes us unfold and expand, and ideas actually begin to grow within us and come to life.

The greatest gifts are new thoughts and unexpected laughter and wisdom.

Do not be afraid to listen to others for fear of what you might hear.

It is who is in your life that matters, not what is in your life.

You should never be ashamed to admit you were wrong—it is only a way of telling somebody that you are a wiser person today than you were yesterday.

You will discover that you will only find your own tranquillity when you are able to discover the fragility and importance of all individual lives.

You are not really listening if you do not listen with your heart.

It is far better for you to control your attitudes and feelings than to have them control you.

One of the greatest forces we can have is the power to listen to others. It provides us with the power to be listened to by others.

Anyone can be a hero, heroism is just a question of doing what has to be done when it needs to be done without considering the consequences.

It is as important to be able to forgive yourself as it is to be forgiven by others.

It is enormously stimulating to *really* listen, to *really* see.

Good credentials don't necessarily make good people.

There are two reasons for being speechless. Either you have not listened to what has been said and therefore have no understanding, or you have listened and understood entirely and need say no more on the subject.

Your background and circumstances at any one time have no bearing upon who or what you can become.

It is better to accept that friends change, than to change friends.

One thing is certain, things must change if they are to get better.

Every living thing grows. There is no life without growth, growth means change and change means growth.

If we insist on living our lives for the future we stand the danger of neglecting the present.

Can you be certain that at this very moment you are not a dragonfly dreaming that you are a person?

Temptation may never pass your way again so think carefully before you decide to resist it.

**In life we wake to sleep
and sleep to wake.**

Learn by going
where you have
to go.

**Failure is a unique method
of being granted another
chance to get it right.**

Accept your fate,
don't waste energy
fighting against
the inevitable.

In life we are many things,
be receptive to the glorious
uncertainty of living.

Those who live to compare themselves with others are likely to be vain and bitter people.

All there are in this world are other people, none are lesser or greater than you.

The most important questions in life must be asked of and answered by oneself.

Yesterday is dead and tomorrow is not yet born. Today is all that matters.

It is a beautiful world despite all it presents us with.

The moment
you think you are
beaten, you are.
The moment you
decide that you will
not be beaten you
are on the path
to victory.

Ordinary can be
turned into the
extraordinary.

Ask yourself whether the result of your life is more important than life.

It is essential to accept responsibility for your life, no one else can do that for you.

There is more than one path in life, and you must be willing to try more than one.

Strive too hard
and you will err.

The problems of life
can only be solved
by allowing yourself
to see beyond them.

**When there are no longer
any answers, questions
must suffice.**

To stop searching is to stop living.

Learning is suddenly understanding something that you've known all your life.

It is never enough to look at a thing once, always try a different perspective.

Do we see all there is to see, or only all that the mind is prepared to comprehend?

We have attempted to make our simple lives even simpler, and have ended up making them a thousand times more complicated.

If a thing
can be
done with
less it is
vanity to
do the
same
thing with
more.

Seek simplicity in all things.

Often the problems that we face in life are impossible to solve purely because the way we have attacked them does not allow for a solution.

It is impossible to separate
yourself from the universe.
You are one and the same.

Accept the importance of balancing
opposites—light and dark, positive and
negative, masculine and feminine—
for they cannot exist alone.

Try being as an infant, knowing nothing except what you hear, see, smell, and feel.

Accept that there are things that cannot be possessed or controlled, air and water cannot be cut or clutched, and their flow ceases when they are enclosed.

You can't put an ocean in your pocket.

Thoughts grow
in brains as grass
grows in fields.

Denying ourselves the right to live life our own way destroys the natural universal harmony— you can't force nature so why force humans when they will harmonize naturally if left to their own devices.

Straightening out life is rather like
trying to push a piece of string or
straightening water.

Take time to observe water
in all the forms it takes, rain,
droplets, trickles, spray,
waves, and torrents.

Live life your own way, and have
the courtesy to allow others to
do the same.

As a plant grows from the seed, expanding from within, so it is with us.

Nature is a whole and only we choose to separate ourselves from the rest of it with labels.

Look closely at individual aspects of the universe and you will discover conflict. But look at the universe as a whole and you will find balance and harmony.

Everything that happens in our lives is our own doing, action or reaction.

Go with the grain,
roll with the punch,
swim with the current,
trim the sails to the wind,
take the tide at flood.

One uses the least amount
of energy in dealing with
a structured life.

Many have wasted a long life. Their lives have been lived in fear of death and in search of some unknown future thing.

Which is more important to you: what you have done or the record of what you have done?

If we can reach a point of trust in ourselves we can move on to trusting others. In order to reach this point we must be prepared to admit our own weaknesses.

Observe cats, how they can sit for hours and just watch, they are not stressed, they do not panic.

Give it a chance and nature will understand you.

Joy and anger occur as naturally as summer and winter.

Let your main desire be the desire not to desire.

Learn to recognize the artificiality of the world of men.

Often the expert is the most poorly equipped to explain the secret of his craft.

He who understands how to deal with circumstances will not allow things to do him harm.

There are those who think that force can achieve anything, in truth, force can achieve very little.

Rules exist to be questioned.

If we can bring ourselves to accept that life is difficult it will no longer matter that it is.

Learn to accept that the process of confronting and solving problems is a painful one.

If there were no problems what need would we have for courage or wisdom?

Often avoiding problems causes more pain than confronting them. Confronting them calls into play our intellect, our courage, and our wisdom. Avoiding them leads only to neurosis.

Accept the necessity
for suffering and the
value of suffering.

Delay gratification.

Accept
responsibility.

**Dedicate yourself
to truth.**

Love is about being able to decide on our values and the relative value that we place on others.

Like children we need reassurance, when we know that we are valued then we feel valuable.

We all want to be made to feel valuable, it is a basic human need.

If we consider ourselves to be valuable we will surely take better care of ourselves, and if we value others, we will take better care of them.

You must learn
to respect others
before you can
respect yourself.

**As much as we'd like
them to, problems do not
just go away.**

Try to avoid seeing life as a matter of can'ts, couldn'ts, and have tos.

Do you see the world, rather than yourself, as the source of your problems?

If you go through life intent on making others miserable, the only person that you will destroy will be yourself.

No problem can be solved until an individual assumes the responsibility for solving it.

By avoiding responsibility you prevent yourself from growing spiritually.

Alter the perspective from which you look at your life, and new possibilities will open up.

At some point during your search for the meaning of life, don't forget to do a little living.

Understanding does not come by way of intellectual study, but through experience.

Once life becomes a habit, we cease to learn.

As we get older it is important that we adapt ourselves to trust the young.

Make your heart laugh and
your sadness will sing.

Everything in life
is just what it seems
to be—there are no
hidden meanings.

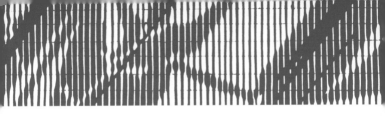

Question with your heart, as well as your head.

The meaning in our life is what each of us brings to it.

Overcome your fears but never stop doubting yourself.

Listen to the opinions of others, but judge by your own standards.

Travel through life as you will, but a heartless path will lead you nowhere.

**See with your mind
as well as your eyes.**

Do not mistake
personality for self.

Society defines success as fame, fortune, and achievement, but you can have all these things and still be a failure if your heart is empty.

Don't put conditions on your happiness, you will never be satisfied.

Endeavor to see all problems as challenges, and all obstacles as an opportunity to prove yourself.

Happiness really does come from within.

On life's journey, our natural feelings of peace, love, and joy frequently become clouded over by negative feelings, chase away those clouds.

Built-up stress and insecurity can be eliminated by rejecting the negative thoughts that engendered them in the first place.

Are we the producers of our thoughts or the victims of them?

Don't let your thoughts take control of your life, take control of them.

Negative feelings tell us that somewhere, something is not right with the way we are dealing with our lives.

Positive feelings tell us we are experiencing life through our natural state of mind, where we have access to our inherent good feelings.

When we can stop judging and start appreciating people's differences, only then can we begin to learn from them.

Allowing negative feelings to persist makes you become like the thing or person you judge or hate, multiplying negativity.

Higher levels of understanding will come naturally from the positive feelings that surface when judgmental thoughts about separate realities are dismissed.

Try to see yourself as others see you, if you don't like what you see, do something about it.

Don't judge anything by external appearances, learn to see beneath the surface.

Tranquillity will only come when you can completely trust your own judgments.

Learn to accept that you are not perfect, nobody is, the important thing is to be aware of where your imperfections lie.

Peace

Speak and think positively—your thoughts, your words, and your deeds will always return to face you.

We are all ultimately responsible for our own actions.

It is important to stand up for what you believe in, but always respect the rights of others to do so too.

Allow your thoughts to go deep into your heart.

Be kind and gentle
in your dealings
with others.

Let your speech be true and your ruling be just.

Aggressive people are always better avoided.

Peace exists within all of us, it is simply waiting to be nurtured and developed.

It is good to laugh often and much.

Try too hard to define that central core of tranquillity that exists within all of us, and it becomes impossible to reach. Accept it and it will always be there to be tapped into.

Don't be satisfied to stay on the first rung of the spiritual ladder forever. Always be prepared to travel onward and upward.

The further mankind gets from his inner truth and energies the more turmoil there is in this world.

Only through personal awareness can we hope to achieve a deep and lasting peace with ourselves.

If you feel that you are right, then you should go ahead and not be afraid.

We can feel we know something and we can feel confident to do something but often we don't know what we're doing.

Thought
is the
source
of power.

**You can be
faithful and
trustworthy,
it is our
natural
impulse to
be honest.**

It is not impossible for you personally to leave the world a slightly better place.

Find ways to put what it is that you know into practice in your daily life or you will become separated from what you know and what you do.

Always strive to see the depth of things, to have the pure, unclouded vision of a child.

The peaceful option is never the easy option, but it is always the way that causes least pain.

If there is a difference between what you observe in spiritual teachings and your daily life, it means that you have not watched and learned well. You do not live with the truth.

It must be your goal to possess the divine qualities of kindness, tolerance, and consideration.

Peace cannot be established on a foundation of fear.

Peace costs nothing but if it is lacking then all the riches in the world are as nothing.

Be ruthless in replacing all old habits which are not based in truth.

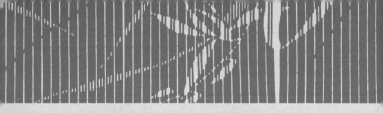

The key to social improvement does not lie in fighting, but in the ability to find solutions that do not involve fighting.

Aggression is blind.

Leaders should never be chosen by the strength of their will alone.

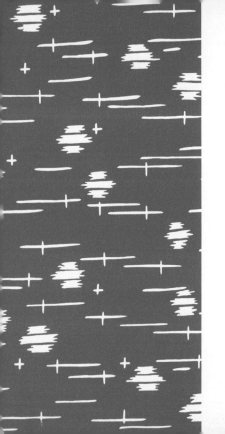

A wise person knows what he should and should not attempt to do.

No one is born brutal or violent, these things must be learned.

A mind left unmanaged is a source of ruin.

Everybody learns to survive one way or the other, but survival is a very different thing to actually living.

Most mistakes come from not harmonizing with the moment, and allowing ourselves to make hasty judgments and ill-considered choices.

It must be our purpose to work toward spiritual balance.

Keep everything in perspective, take a deep breath, and think peaceful thoughts.

The start of something new always brings with it the hope of something great. It's a wonderful feeling.

Attune the mind and spirit to a proper perspective.

Do not allow yourself to become jaded by experience and disappointment, always strive to retain your enthusiasm and energy for the new.

You must listen to your own heart, for it will never lie to you.

A good teacher accentuates the positive.

You will discover that it is important to believe in the path we have chosen even when others can't see where we are going.

Too many people do nothing to develop their self-contained spiritual qualities, meanwhile they seek divine help externally.

Don't expect others to give you what you would not be prepared to part with yourself.

The true spiritual teacher is one's own developed spiritual energy.

Without proper commitment to the right path, you will deviate from it.

The growth of spiritual self-consciousness is what enables people to be responsible in their lives.

Whatever evil one does to others, is ultimately done to oneself. Realize this and live in peace with the world.

Never take peace for granted, it is never as valued as when it is absent.

The true importance of the soul lies in its association with everyday life.

**Negative attitudes and selfish
behavior are the enemies of
personal peace.**

The fruit one bears in one's life depends
entirely on how you live each day.

**Peace, harmony, and quietude
are the foundation upon which
life can survive.**

When you choose your teacher, look carefully at how they live as well as how much they know.

Words are often inadequate to describe the truth of something.

Words can all too easily be misinterpreted—make sure you say what you think you are saying.

Understand that your material life is only a small part of your whole life.

Allow your spiritual reality to shape your material situation.

Unless you make the effort yourself, no one in heaven or on earth can help you.

Peace cannot be imposed on you,
it must come from within.

Develop a rich inner life, our
own internal world sustains
our health and keeps us in
touch with our spiritual reality.

No one can cheat
anyone except
himself.

Always be self-critical, but don't forget to offer praise too when you deserve it.

No one can be said to be either completely good or completely bad, we all have the potential to be better or worse than we are.

To make any progress toward peace you must be prepared to face challenges. Peace is not about turning away from problems.

Try to consciously "un-learn" any bad habits that you have acquired.

Accept that everyday life will not always make you feel good, strong, and positive.

Life won't always encourage the upward movement of your energy.

Don't be the victim of your own moods.

Violent mood swings cannot exist in a peaceful mind.

Moods are a clear indicator of the burden that is being placed on the health of our body and soul.

Physical life has cycles. Allow yourself to relax into these.

How you manage each moment of the precious opportunity of life is an expression of your true being.

Quiet contemplation is a good antidote to the stresses of the day.

Meditation can help us to depart from the general busy activities of the mind to a quieter, more ordered sphere.

One should never bring a troubled mind to meditative sitting.

Honesty is a state of mind.

Inner peace is the ultimate self-confidence.

Troubled thoughts and unresolved problems cannot live in a peaceful mind.

Consciousness is that annoying time between naps.

We enter this world naked, wet, and hungry—things can only get better.

Give the world the best you have,
and it may never be enough.
Give the world the best you've
got anyway.

**People will forget tomorrow
the good you do today.
Do good anyway.**

If you find serenity and happiness,
do not gloat over it and try to make
others jealous. If you do these
things then you have not really
found serenity and happiness.

We lock ourselves into the paranoia that what we make others will destroy, so often we do nothing when we should just go ahead.

Success brings false friends and truer enemies.

When we are kind many wonder what our motives are.

People are often unreasonable, illogical, and self-centered. Forgive them anyway.

The way to peace is easier than you think.

Laughter is the only true antidote to grief.

Dreams can sometimes be more powerful than facts.

Myth can sometimes be more potent than history.

In life you can never find out how far it is possible for you to go without taking some risk.

Use the stones that life throws at you to lay the foundations for your future.

Have the courage to dream the impossible dream.

If you don't like failure, try again— and keep trying.

Make good use of each day. One man's week is another man's year.

Ambition never gets anywhere by itself.

Poverty might steal your fine clothes but it can't steal your laughter.

Cherish the music that stirs in your heart.

**Stick to
your ideals.**

Trust your
own vision.

Live your own life— follow your own star.

Set your own patterns in life.

Even if you are certain of your path, always be open to the advice of others—you never stop learning.

Dare to be different.

Champion the right to be yourself.

Can you be alone
with yourself? And
do you truly like the
company you keep
in the empty
moments?

When all else falls away, it doesn't matter where you live or how much money you have.

Age is irrelevant—peace is not the preserve of the elderly or sedate.

It doesn't interest me what you do for a living, it is how you conduct yourself while you do it that counts.

**Make peace not only your goal,
but also your way of living.**

Care less for your harvest than for how it
is shared, and your life will have meaning
and your heart will have peace.

To withhold is to wither.

To give is to love.

Peace is the most positive environment for growth of mind and spirit. In your dealing with others look past your differences.

What is peace but the absence of anger and anxiety?

Inner peace is about having balanced emotions and coming to terms with the vicissitudes of life.

You will discover that life is confusing and filled with turmoil, accept that and hold fast to peace.

Peace is about coming to terms with your physical nature.

Peace is about common sense, information, rationale, and clarity.

Peace comes with will power and intelligence.

Peace will be ours when we allow tranquillity into our lives.

You cannot force peace on another, persuade by example.

You will discover that,
whatever you thought before,
you are a child of the universe
and like the stars in the sky or
the trees in the park, you
have a right to be here.

Tranquillity
Lost

It is far easier with some to find fault than it is for them to do the task themselves.

Never criticize something that you are not willing to do yourself.

When you think you can't go on, you will be able to keep going.

Knowledge lasts a lifetime, charm will work only for minutes.

Those who talk often
do not know.

It is okay to feel angry.

It is never right to be cruel.

Your background and your circumstances at any time have no bearing upon who you can become.

Ought = duty

Try = will

Won't = defeat

Can = power

Did = achievement

Those closest to us will hurt us from time to time, as we will hurt them. Make apologies well in advance.

Some secrets are better kept secret.

It is vital to remain interested in your own career no matter how humble or disjointed it may seem.

The world is full of trickery, it is wise to exercise caution but don't neglect to enjoy the show.

The enlightened rarely make a show,
the self-righteous are rarely respected,
boasters achieve little and braggarts
will not endure.

**The biggest thief of time is
procrastination.**

Don't expect the impossible of
yourself—there are limitations to
being human.

You are not perfect.
None of us are.

Learn to respect your weaknesses and to make the most of your strengths.

You are
capable
of doing
something
that makes
a difference.

It is no use blaming fate for failures, or pinning success onto luck.

Almost anything is possible, but remember the almost.

Those who want to succeed will surely find a way, and those who don't will find an excuse.

It is always useful to know what you are about.

No one who takes part is a loser.

Your conscience will not prevent sin—it exists to prevent you from enjoying it.

Those who insist upon doing all the talking themselves are poor listeners.

Instead of listening to what is being said to them, many listen instead to what they are going to say.

Allow yourself some quiet time for meditation.

It is important to make the opportunity to revise your time management and allow yourself to break bad habits.

Never underestimate the importance of play.

Sleep is important.
Don't ignore your
body's needs.

**Smile and laugh more.
It helps to lighten your
emotional load.**

Count your blessings daily.

Don't be ashamed to think a few nice thoughts about yourself occasionally.

Simplify your life.

Make sure that the goals you set yourself are realistic.

Develop a sense of purpose.

Learn to forgive.

Strive to be optimistic and allow your expectations to become positive.

Don't count on anybody else coming along to relieve your stress.

**You are in charge of managing
your own pressure.**

You are the only one who will,
or even can, do much to lighten
your psychological load.

Something as simple as a relaxing bath can work wonders to restore tranquillity.

Worry gives a small thing a big shadow.
                              Swedish proverb

Nothing can change unless we are prepared to actively tackle it.

Focus on
what it is
you want
in your life.

Don't ignore the things that give you real pleasure.

Quality is never accidental.

Always apologize when you have been wrong.

A bit of fragrance always clings to the hand that gives you roses.

Chinese proverb

The highest reward for work is not what you get for it, but what you become by it.

Your actions may not always bring you happiness, but there can be no happiness without action.

Doubt cramps energy.

Attitude is a little thing that
makes a big difference.

Attitudes are contagious.

If you do not believe in yourself the chances are that nobody else will.

We all have the capacity to learn from the mistakes of others and yet we remain reluctant to do so.

It is amazing just how good you feel after you have encouraged someone else.

Don't ever miss the opportunity to say something positive.

No one means all they say, and very few say all they mean.

Words are slippery.

Facts are stubborn things, they cannot be ignored.

It is easier to fight for one's principles than to live up to them.

Don't blame others or you will have to give up your power to change.

If only once we had found ourselves we could lose our memory.

Imagine the extent of our freedom if we were to put aside those things that we feel limit us.

No one can learn
from someone that
they do not respect.

**Nobody can be exactly like you,
learn to accept and love your
uniqueness.**

There are those that see everything they do as a thankless chore, and there are those who do all that is required of them with a positive attitude. Nothing they do is a chore but an act of will.

We cease to be truly alive when regret takes the place of dreams.

It is no good
being able to read
music if you are
unable to feel it.

**Everything that we say
we feel is important, is
important.**

Words are often inadequate
to communicate all that we
feel in our hearts.

**Don't waste time, for
if we lose present time
then we lose all time.**

If you know where you are going—
you will surely arrive. If you don't know
where you are going—you will surely end
up somewhere else.

Solitude is not a place to settle.

No bird flies with another's wings, and
no bird can soar too high with its own.

Prediction is
difficult, and
more often
than not,
impossible.

Use your eyes. Sometimes those who offer us eternal salvation surround themselves with dead plants.

History is made up of truths and lies in unequal proportion.

**While you are killing time
remember that time is killing you.**

Those who are fortunate to
have been born with two eyes
should never view life through
just one.

Death should not be feared half as much as living an inadequate life.

If only our impulse to create could match our impulse to possess.

About all you can do in life
is be who you are.

**Value those people who
love you for yourself.**

Beware of those
who only love you
for what you can
do for them.

Accept that there will always be some people that won't like you.

Truth should not be something that hurts the teller.

Never be ashamed of who you are.

Truth is always exciting.

Life becomes dull and tedious when isolated from the truth.

Distrust anything
that compels you to
forfeit your liberty.

**Only you can change
your life.**

If you want time make time.
You will never find time.

**Always try to finish what
you begin.**

Bliss is the icing on the cake.
Enjoy it.

Experience is not something that we can create, it is something that we must undergo.

The person who insists they have no faults is a liar.

Despite what others think you are, be what you are.

Before getting bogged down and depressed about what you are, consider what you have the potential to become.

Allow yourself the time and space to grow into your ambitions.

Although it is admirable to be wiser than others, it is definitely unwise to tell them.

We can go through life cursing the darkness, or we can simply light a candle.

War or peace? Is it really such a difficult choice?

The person who can speak equally well of every other person can equally well speak ill of just as many.

No forged metal can form a chain capable of fettering the mind.

The easiest way of getting the measure of a person is to analyze their enemies.

Begin to enjoy your doubts—see them as challenges.

Those who love most have parted most.

The history of all mankind is there to be had—pickled in quotations.

Event minus the impossible equals truth.

The wise have a truer perception of how ignorant they are. Those who are not wise will never discover this.

Those seeking to astound themselves should do the things they are capable of doing.

A life lived for others is a life with meaning.

Tranquillity is the easiest thing to lose.

Nature cannot be cheated, don't try.

Tranquillity comes with a healthy body and soul.

Embrace the challenges of life, you must want to succeed, but beware of wanting anything too much.

When you are happy with yourself and the world around you, only then can you expect to start on the path to tranquillity.

Life Is A Challenge—Meet It!
Life Is A Song—Sing It!
Life Is A Dream—Realize It!
Life Is A Game—Play It!
Life Is Love—Enjoy It!

Bhagawan Sri Sathya Sai Baba

Published in 2000 by
Sourcebooks, Inc
1935 Brookdale Road, Suite 139
Naperville IL 60563

Text © David Baird 2000
Design concept: Broadbase
Design: Philippa Jarvis

Printed and bound in Spain

MQ 10 9 8 7 6 5 4 3

ISBN: 1-57071-527-0